FIT LIKE?

How are you?

First published in the United Kingdom in 2013 by Robert Gordon University, Garthdee House, Garthdee Road, Aberdeen, AB10 7QB.

Robert Gordon University is a Scottish charity registered under charity number SC013781.

Designed and compiled by Karen Barrett-Ayres.

ISBN number 978-1-907349-07-2

INTRODUCTION   02
THE BASICS   04
PEOPLE   12
SMALL TALK   14
SOCIALISING   18
EATING & DRINKING 20
THE WEATHER   22
CLOTHING   24
ANATOMY   26
ACTIONS   29
ANIMALS   30
FURTHER STUDY   32

INTRODUCTION

FIT'S THIS AA ABOOT EN?
What's this all about then?

Doric is a Scottish dialect spoken in the North East of Scotland around Aberdeen city and shire.

The term 'Doric' is thought to come from the Greek for 'rural' or 'rustic' perhaps due to its strong associations with the farming and fishing communities of the region.

There is an extensive body of literature, poetry, ballads and songs from the North East.

In the Disney animation 'Brave', a character speaks Doric and there's a running joke that nobody can understand him. The voice actor was Kevin McKidd, a native of Elgin. Although Doric is the traditional dialect of the North East, don't worry, we do all speak English!

FAR ABOOTS DIV THE' SPIK IT?

In which areas is it spoken?

LOSSIEMOUTH

ELGIN

BUCKIE

FOCHABERS

MACDUFF

FRASERBURGH
(The Broch)

NEW PITSLIGO

KEITH

TURRIFF
(Turra)

ABERLOUR

PETERHEAD

HUNTLY

METHLICK

INSCH

OLDMELDRUM

ELLON

INVERURIE

TOMINTOUL

ALFORD

KEMNAY

BRAEMAR

BALLATER

ABOYNE

TORPHINS

ABERDEEN
(Aiberdeen)

STONEHAVEN

LAURENCEKIRK

MONTROSE

THE BASICS

SO FOO DIV YE SPIK I' DORIC?
So how do you speak Doric?

Doric words can differ from town to town. If you're from Peterhead, you might refer to a seagull as a 'pyool' but in Aberdeen, the same bird would be known as a 'scurry'. And in Buckie it's a 'gow'.

There are also many variations on the spellings of the words, due to differences of localised pronunciation and phonetics. The word 'Pyool' for instance could also be written as 'pule', 'pool' or 'pyewel' depending on which town you are from.

PETERHEAD SEAGULL

PYOOL

SCURRY

ABERDEEN CITY SEAGULL

AYE ➡ YES

AYE, AYE! ➡ HELLO!

NAE ➡ NO

I DA KEN ➡ I DON'T KNOW

NAE BITHER ➡ IT'S NO TROUBLE

DIV YE KEN? ➡ DO YOU KNOW?

USING THE 'F' WORD

Try switching 'wh' with 'f'

FAR? Where?

Basic phonology
'Wh' at the beginning of words is often realised as an 'f'.

FIT? What?

FAN? When?

FOO? How?

FIT WYE? Why?

FA? Who?

Far ye gaan?
Where are you going?

← **FAR** →

Far div ye bide?
Where do you stay?

Fit's at?
What's that?

← **FIT** →

Fit like?
(What like?)
How are you?

Fan ye aff?
When are you going?

← **FAN** →

Fan div ye yoke?
When do you start work?

Foo mony?
How many?

← **FOO** →

Foo's yer doos?
(How are your doves/pigeons?)
How are you?

Fa's at?
Who is that?

← **FA** →

Fa's roond is it?
Whose turn is it to buy the drinks?

Fit wye nae?
Why not?

← **FIT WYE** →

Fit wye's at noo?
Why is that now?

COLOURS

REID	Red
YALLA	Yellow
BLAE	Blue
FITE	White
BLAIK	Black
BROON	Brown
SILLER	Silver
SKYRIE	Gaudy/showy

NUMBERS

MONY A MICKLE MAAKS A MUCKLE
Many small amounts together becomes a large amount

Een: One
I'll hae at een, cheers
I'll have that one, thanks

Twa: Two
Twa craws sat upon a wa
Two crows sat upon a wall

Fower: Four
Atween fleers een an fower
Between floors one and four

Hillock: Lots
At's a fair hillock o' chips
That's a lot of chips

Foo muckle? How much?
Foo muckle is at?
How much is that?

Bourachie: A group/huddle
A bourachie o' bairns
A bunch of kids

1 EEN

2 TWA

THREE

4 FOWER

3

6

SEIVEN 7

SAX

EEN

5

11

8 ECHT

9 NINE

10 TEN

FIVE

ELEEVEN

12 TWAL/ DIZZEN

OPPOSITES

MUCKLE	Big	Small	**SMA**
GYE BIG	Large	Little	**WEE**
AA	All	None	**NEEN**
AAWYE	Everywhere	Nowhere	**NAEWYE**
AATHIN	Everything	Nothing	**NITHIN**
AABODY	Everyone	Nobody	**NAEBODY**

Doric	English		English	Doric
UP	Up		Down	DOON
GING IN	Go in		Go out	GING OOT
OWER	Over		Above	ABEEN
AROON	Around		About	ABOOT
AHEID	Ahead		Behind	AHIN
AFORE	Before		After	AIFTER

PEOPLE

MANNIE

Man

Check at
mannie's fisog!
Look at that
man's face!

WIFIE

Woman

At wifie Fraser's
a richt blether
That Fraser
woman talks a lot

LOON

Boy/son

Far's the loon
i'day?
Where is your
son today?

QUINE

Girl/daughter

Fit a bonny
wee quine
What a pretty
little girl

GEETS

Children

Fit a hillock
o' geets
What a lot
of children

BAIRNS

Children

Foo mony bairns
are in i' playgrun?
How many kids are
in the playground?

TOONSER
Lives in the city

TEUCHTER
A rural dweller

Boyfriend

Girlfriend

Blaa: boast
He's ayeways blaain
aboot his new car
He's always boasting
about his new car

Crabbit: Bad tempered
He's affa crabbit i'day
He's really grumpy today

Claik: Gossip
Funcy a fly cup and a claik?
Fancy a sneaky cup of tea
and a gossip?

Clype: To tell tales
Dinna clype te mannie Broon
Don't tell tales to Mr Brown

Footer: Messing about
Quit footerin aboot!
Stop messing about!

Grippy: Miserley
He's affa grippy wi his siller
He's very miserly with
his money

Swaak: Agile
He's a swaak loon
He's an agile boy

Swick: To cheat
He' min, stop swickin in!
Hey, stop jumping the queue!

Sook: Sycophant
She's a richt sook
She's a right flatterer

SMALL TALK

> **Aye, aye fit like en Jim? Are ye nae spikin? Foo's the wife an geets?**

Hello, how are you Jim? Are you not speaking? How's the wife and kids?

> **Nae bad Mary – chavin awa. They're aa fine, cheers. Fit aboot yersel?**

I'm not too bad Mary – doing okay. They're all fine, thanks. What about you?

> **I'm fair-tricket! Dod's just booked us a wee holiday so we're awa tae Tenerife!**

I'm delighted! George has just booked a short holiday, so we're off to Tenerife!

> **Oh fit fine! At Dod's a fine chiel ye ken! Fan ye gaan awa?**

How lovely! George is a nice fellow you know! When are you going away?

> **I' morn's morn – I'm nae packed so I'll need tae ging hame an maak a stairt.**

Tomorrow morning – I'm not packed so I'll need to go home and make a start.

> **Aye, nae bithir. Well hae a rare time an mind an pack yer dookers!**

No problem. Well have a great time and remember your swimming costume!

FIT I DINNA KEN IS NAE WURTH KENNIN.

I am very knowledgeable and a know-it-all.

TIME

ONYTIME I'DAY WOULD BE NICE

I'day: today

THE NOO

Right now

FIT YE DEEIN THIS AIFTERNEEN?

Aifterneen: afternoon

NEXT WIK

Next week

SEE YE THE MORN'S MORN

Tomorrow morning

POSITIVE EMOTIONS

Bosie: hug
Gie's a bosie!
Give me a hug!

Fash: trouble
Dinna fash yersel
Don't trouble yourself

Tricket: Delighted
I'm fair-tricket
I'm delighted

Gawaaah!: Get away!
Gawaaah! Yer kiddin!
Get away! You're kidding me!

Bonny: beautiful
Sheena is affa bonny
Sheena is very pretty

Fine: good
Affa fine butteries
Very tasty pastries

Rare: great
It's bin a rare nicht oot
It's been a great night out

NEGATIVE EMOTIONS

Scunnered: fed up
I'm affa scunnered
I'm really fed up

Greetin: crying
Fit ye greetin fur?
Why are you crying?

Wheesht: quiet
Hud yer wheesht!
Be quiet!

Spikin: speaking
Are ye nae spikin?
Are you not speaking to me?

Weel: well
Am nae weel
I'm not feeling well

Forfauchan: exhausted
I'm affa forfauchan!
I'm really exhausted!

Puggled: tired
I'm fair puggled the day
I'm really tired today

Neep: turnip
Yer a neep
You are an idiot

Gype: fool
Fit a gype
What a fool

Glaikit: senseless, stupid
At loon's a bit glaikit
That boy is a bit stupid

Bile: boil
Awa an bile yer heid!
Go away!

Mingin: not pleasant
At baps are mingin
Those rolls are not pleasant

Feart: scared
Dinna be feart
Don't be scared

Coorse: nasty
She's a coorse besom*
She's a nasty woman
(*a besom is also a broomstick)

SOCIALISING

COME AWA' BEN THE HOOSE

Welcome, come through

YE WINTIN' A FLY AN' A PIECE?

Would you like a cup of tea and something to eat?

TAAK A PEW/ SIT YERSEL DOON

Take a seat/sit down

SO FIT HIV YE BIN UP TAE?

So what have you been up to?

AN FOOS YER MA 'N' DA?

And how are your mother and father?

AN FAR YE BIDIN THE NOO?

And where are you living at the moment?

YE GAAN OOT? INTAE TOON?

Are you heading out this evening? Into the city centre?

AYE, FAR AND FAN WILL I SEE YE?

Yes, where and when will we meet?

FUNCY A DUNCE/ ARE YE DUNCIN?

Would you like to dance?

NO YER AARICHT I'M WABBIT!

No thanks, I'm exhausted!

FIT YE HAEIN?

What are having to drink?

I'LL HAE A PINT. CHEERS MIN!

I'll have a pint. Good health!

EATING & DRINKING

A FLY CUP
A cup of tea

SCOOF IT!
Drink up!

NEEPS & TATTIES
Turnips and potatoes

A CAPPIE
Ice-cream cone

SPEEN Spoon

BUTTERY OR ROWIE
A flat breakfast pastry

HINGIN INGINS
Hanging onions

SPROOTS
Sprouts

Clootie: cloth
Gee at worktop a dicht wi a clootie
Give that worktop a wipe with a cloth

GALSHIKS
Sweeties

Messages: shopping
I'm awa te dee my messages

Chipper: chip shop
Ye needin onything fae the chipper?

BRAMMLE
Blackberry

A FUNCY PIECE
A cake or sweet treat

Fine: tasty
Affa fine butteries
Very tasty pastries

Sappy: juicy
Is peach is affa sappy
This peach is really juicy

Aet: feed
At wiz a gweed aet
That was a nice meal

Gads: yuk
Gads min!
Yuk!

Bowfin': disgusting
At soup's bowfin'
That soup is disgusting

Mingin': horrible
At pie's mingin'
That pie is horrible

Fooshty: gone bad/rotten
At bap's are fooshty
Those rolls are mouldy

Cowk: retch/feel sick
At milks maakin' me cowk
That milk is making me sick

DORIC IDIOMS

AM NAE AS GREEN AS
AM CUBBIGE LOOKIN

I'm not as green as I am
cabbage looking...
I'm not as stupid as I look

IT'S A SARE FECHT
FIR HALF A LOAF

It's a sore fight for a half loaf...
It's hard to make ends meet

THE WEATHER

IT'S GYE WAREM I'DAY

It's very hot today

IT'S A BIT DREICH I'DAY

It's a bit dull today

IT'S AYE DINGIN DOON

It's a long spell of rain

FIT A BONNY GLOAMIN'

What a pretty sunset

IT'S CAUL I'DAY

It's cold today

HAP UP YER LUGS

Cover up your ears

I'M DROOKIT
I'm soaked

CA CANNY, OR YOU'LL GING SKITIN'
Take care, it's a bit icy

IT'S BLOWIN' A HOOLIE
It's very windy

FEELS LIKE SNA
Feels like it's going to snow

THE HAARS COMIN' IN
There's a sea fog descending

MY BEETS ARE DUBBY
My boots are muddy

CLOTHING
(CLAES)

TOURIE
Hat

GLAESSES
Glasses

Shirt
SARK

GANZIE
Jumper

SIMMIT
Vest

BUG
Bag

BREEKS
Trousers

GYMMIES
Plimsolls

PINTS
Laces

PUNTS/DRAWERS
Underwear

FIT A RARE BUNNET

What a nice hat

AT'S SOME RIG-OOT YE HIV ON THE NICHT

That's some outfit you have on tonight

FAR DID YE GET YER FUNCY SHEEN FAE?

Where did you get your fancy shoes from?

BUNNET
Flat cap

HUMMEL DODDIES
Fingerless gloves

STOCKIN SOLES
Socks

SHEEN/SHEE
Shoes/shoe

ANATOMY

THESE INGINS ARE FAIR MAAKIN MY EEN WAATER

These onions are really making my eyes water

AT POKED ME RICHT IN THE EE

That poked me right in the eye

MY QUEETS HIV SWAALT

I've got swollen ankles

FIT FIT FITS FIT FIT?

Which foot fits which foot?

I CANNA FEEL MY TAES

I can't feel my toes

HE'S AN AFFA KYTE ON HIM

He has a big stomach on him

KEEP YER LUGS WAARM

Keep your ears warm

STOP LUGGIN IN

Stop eavesdropping

HE KITTLED MA OXTERS

He tickled my armpits

SHE SKELPT HIS DOWP

She slapped his bum

I'VE AFFA SAIR BEANS I'DAY

My bones are aching today

DOON IN THE MOO

Down in the mouth / sad

HE SPIKS WI A BOOL IN HIS MOO

He talks with a posh accent

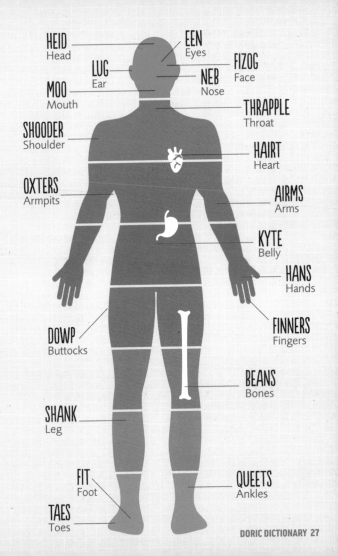

HEID
Head

EEN
Eyes

LUG
Ear

FIZOG
Face

NEB
Nose

MOO
Mouth

THRAPPLE
Throat

SHOODER
Shoulder

HAIRT
Heart

OXTERS
Armpits

AIRMS
Arms

KYTE
Belly

HANS
Hands

DOWP
Buttocks

FINNERS
Fingers

BEANS
Bones

SHANK
Leg

FIT
Foot

QUEETS
Ankles

TAES
Toes

YER LOOKIN AFFA PEELIE-WALLY. FIT'S A DEE?

You look a bit off colour. What's wrong with you?

ACTIONS

Div: To do
Fit div yi dee for a bite o met?
What do you do for a living?

Ging: To go
Ging up i' stairs
Go up the stairs

Gang: To go
Ye may gang far and fare waur
You may go a lot further and
do a lot worse

Hing: To hang
Fit wye are ye hingin aboot?
Why are you hanging about?

Hud: To hold
Shut yer een and hud on
Shut your eyes and hold on

Taak: To take
Taak it hame wi ye
Take it home with you

Teen: Taken
She's been teen te A&E
She's been taken to
Accident and Emergency

Rug: To pull
I'm ruggin it as hard as I can
I'm pulling it as hard as I can

Gaar: To cause, to make
The reek o his taes gaared
me bowk
The stink of his toes made
me be sick

Howk: To scratch, swipe
He howked his ba ower
the wa
He swiped his ball over
the wall

Dirl: To spin
He dirled her aboot
the dunce fleer
He spun her about
the dance floor

Lowp: to jump
Awa an taak a lowp!
Away and take a jump!

ANIMALS
(CRAITERS)

SANDY'S AN
AFFA PEER CRAITER
I feel sorry for Sandy

RUBBIT
Rabbit

TOD
Fox

SHILT/SHILTIE
Horse

DUG
Dog

KITTLEN
Kitten

MOOSE
Mouse

YOWE
Ewe

COO/BEAST
Cow

Sharn: Cow dung
Yer beets are clarted in sharn
Your boots are covered in
cow dung

**Knapdarlochs: matted
dung on the hind-quarters
of cattle or sheep**
Yer gimmer has knapdarlochs
Your ewe with one lamb
has matted dung on her wool

BIRDS

OOLET
Owl

SWALLA
Swallow

SCURRY/PYOOL/GOW
Seagull

TARIK
Arctic Tern

CRAW
Crow

COOSHIE DOO
Pigeon

DEUK/JOOK
Duck

SPUGGIE
Sparrow

BUBBLYJOCK
Turkey

TAMMIE NORRIE
Puffin

SCRATH
Cormorant

INSECTS

FOGGY BUMMER
Bumble bee

WURREM
Worm

GOLLACH
Beetle

FLECH
Flea

FURTHER STUDY

WANT TE KEN MAIR?
Want to know more?

The best way to learn Doric is to visit Aberdeen and the North East of Scotland and listen to the locals speaking it, especially in the more rural areas.

Why not visit our riverside campus at Garthdee in Aberdeen and say 'Fit like!'

If you're keen to learn more, there are a wide range of websites and resources available online, including www.doricdictionary.com and facebook.com/wespikdoric.

You can also visit the RGU website:

www.rgu.ac.uk/local-lingo

Robert Gordon University in Aberdeen is a top-rated university for employability.

We do of course deliver all of our flexible courses in English!

Discover our courses at:
www.rgu.ac.uk